Moving Through
Dimensions

a mathematics unit for high-ability learners in grades 6–8

Moving Through
Dimensions

The College of William and Mary
School of Education
Center for Gifted Education
P.O. Box 8795
Williamsburg, Virginia 23187

Center for Gifted Education Staff:
Executive Director: Dr. Joyce VanTassel-Baska
Director: Dr. Janice I. Robbins
Curriculum Director: Dr. Kimberley L. Chandler
Curriculum Writer: Dana T. Johnson
Unit Reviewer: Dr. Susan G. Assouline

Edited by Lacy Compton
Production Design by Marjorie Parker

ISBN-13: 978-1-59363-390-5
ISBN-10: 1-59363-390-4

Prufrock Press Inc.
P.O. Box 8813
Waco, TX 76714-8813
Phone: (800) 998-2208
Fax: (800) 240-0333
http://www.prufrock.com

Contents

Part I: Introduction to the Unit

Introduction to the Unit

Unit Introduction: *Moving Through Dimensions* approaches spatial reasoning through one-dimensional (1-D), two-dimensional (2-D), and three-dimensional (3-D) tasks. Students explore the transition between dimensions and representations of three-dimensional objects in two dimensions.

Unit Rationale: All students need to develop good spatial reasoning skills. However, gifted students are more likely to demonstrate an aptitude for advanced spatial reasoning at an early age. They also are more likely to enroll in later programs that require advanced math and science knowledge and skills. These courses often serve as a gatekeeper to certain college majors and career opportunities. Because gifted students tend to respond to spatial reasoning experiences so well, they need more of them, both in quantity and complexity, than the standard curriculum provides. This unit will help them understand material in courses beyond middle school. Science courses and higher level mathematics courses require spatial reasoning. Careers in engineering, architecture, medicine, and the sciences require visualizing relationships that are spatial in nature. Some of these relationships cannot be experienced directly but must be manipulated in the mind. Here are some examples:

- In geometry, to find the diagonal length of a shoebox, one is finding the length of a segment that is the hypotenuse of an invisible right triangle.
- In the sciences, molecular structure cannot be observed directly, but the relationships of the atoms need to be understood. Two-dimensional models of these three-dimensional objects often are used.
- The entrance exam for dental school (Dental Admissions Test) has a section called Perceptual Ability that requires interpretation of information about 3-D objects that is given in two dimensions.
- When a surgeon reads an MRI, he or she needs to transfer the collection of two-dimensional images he or she sees into an understanding of a three-dimensional organ or body part.

These skills need to be developed over many years. By beginning in elementary school and continuing in this middle school unit, these students will be better prepared for experiences such as geometry and physical science, which will build toward high school and college coursework in mathematics, science, and engineering.

This unit will help develop an aptitude for spatial reasoning that already is present in some gifted students. It will offer opportunities that correspond to their demonstrated interests and aptitudes. It may be an awakening point for students who have not had these interests sparked due to lack of prior experiences.

Unit Goals:

Goal 1: To understand the role of one, two, and three dimensions in the physical world. Students will be able to:
- identify the number of dimensions that are needed to contain or represent various objects in the real world.

Goal 2: To develop skills in spatial reasoning. Students will be able to:
- create two-dimensional representations of three-dimensional objects, including perspective drawings, projections, cross-section diagrams, and mat plans;

- construct or describe three-dimensional objects based on information given in two dimensions; and
- construct and analyze fractal patterns.

Goal 3: To develop problem-solving skills in problems that require understanding of spatial relationships. Students will be able to:
- solve problems that require reasoning about objects that they cannot experience directly; and
- solve problems that require finding all variations on an arrangement of geometric patterns in two or three dimensions.

Differentiation for Gifted Learners: The experiences that are suggested in this unit can be beneficial to all students. However, they are designed with the special needs of gifted students in mind. Reasons to use this unit with gifted learners include the following:

- The regular school curriculum does not provide many experiences necessary to develop spatial reasoning skills fully. This unit provides some additional experiences.
- Spatial tasks can provide a level of abstraction that is challenging to gifted learners as they will need to manipulate mental images.
- Ideas are introduced that will support later higher level coursework. For example, high school geometry requires students to recognize congruent figures and their corresponding parts in order to do congruence proofs. The idea of finding volume by slicing is introduced; this is a technique that is used in calculus. The physical sciences require visualizing 3-D structures of things such as atoms and crystals.
- Higher level questions are included.
- Written explanations are required rather than only giving numerical answers to questions. Writing reinforces analytical and reflective thinking.
- The task demands are more rigorous than in typical curriculum materials. Students are sometimes asked to complete tasks with less teacher support than would be given in a typical math class.
- The vocabulary used in student handouts assumes strong verbal skills.
- There is a large amount of mathematical content included in this unit, which is covered in an accelerated time frame.
- Suggested extension activities allow the unit to be tailored according to the individual abilities of students.
- Much of the work in this unit is inquiry based. Although this approach may benefit all students, inquiry lessons are an excellent way to unleash the thinking abilities of gifted students.
- Appropriate problem-solving challenges are posed for mathematically gifted students.

Suggested Grade Level Range: 6–8

Prerequisite Knowledge: Students should be familiar with perimeter, area, volume of a cylinder, and volume of a cone.

Length of Lessons: The length of lessons can be adjusted by selecting or omitting various activities. A number of the lessons will take more than one 50- to 60-minute class session. There are a number of extensions that can be used at other times during the school year for continued work in spatial reasoning.

Timing: This unit can be completed in eight lessons or spread throughout the semester. It may be used in a pull-out or enrichment class. Not all lessons need to

Table 1

Suggestions for Implementing Lessons

Minimum Treatment of This Unit	Intermediate Treatment of This Unit	Maximum Treatment of This Unit
• Younger students (grade 6 and below). • Limited time frame. • Students need more support.	• Grade 6 students who are new to this kind of material. • Fewer than seven class periods available.	• More than seven class periods available. • Grades 7 or 8. • Students are very capable.
• Lessons 1, 2, 4, 5, 7, and 9. • Be selective about activities within the lessons. Adapt questions as needed and minimize writing activities.	• Lessons 1, 2, 3, 4, 5, 7, and 9. • Do only the easier extensions.	• All lessons and some extensions. • Assign some independent extensions.
• Align the pre- and postassessment questions to match what will be covered in the selected lessons.	• Align the pre- and postassessment questions to match what will be covered in the selected lessons.	• Do all assessment questions.

be included. The order of lessons may be determined by the teacher. Table 1 gives suggestions for selecting lessons for various classroom needs.

Extensions: Suggestions for extension activities are included within lessons and at the end of the unit. Some can be done either by groups or by individuals. You also might keep a piece of poster paper hanging in your classroom and encourage students to generate questions regarding material they want to know more about; individuals or groups can be asked to find answers and report back as additional extensions. The extensions often require students to function somewhat independently. However, you may choose to assign extensions to less able students by writing a more scaffolded version of the task.

Assessment: Each lesson has suggested assessments, but teachers may find additional ways to determine student understanding.

Journals: If students maintain a math journal, they can be asked to solve assigned problems in their journals and explain their reasoning. A good technique to create an audience for student writing is to suggest that they write a postcard to a friend who has asked for help in solving the problem. Suggested journal prompts are included in some of the lessons.

Preassessment: This is not a readiness test. It is intended to give you a baseline indicator of what students know before they start the unit. If some students perform well on the preassessment, you should use the lessons and unit extensions to extend their learning.

Postassessment: This is included at the end of the unit. It is parallel in structure to the preassessment. If you administer both instruments, you will be able to tell if students learned the concepts as a result of participating in this unit.

Glossary

Fractal: A geometric shape that can be split into parts, each of which is (at least approximately) a reduced-size copy of the whole.

Iteration: One cycle of a set of instructions to be repeated.

Self-similarity: An object is similar to a part of itself; the whole has the same shape as one or more of the parts.

Part II: Lesson Plans

Lesson Plans

Lesson 1: Preassessment
Lesson 2: Introduction to Dimensions
Lesson 3: Drawing Cube Structures
Lesson 4: Projecting Through Dimensions
Lesson 5: Polycubes
Lesson 6: Slices
Lesson 7: Solids of Revolution
Lesson 8: Sierpinski Triangle and Pyramid
Lesson 9: Postassessment

Lesson 1: Preassessment

Instructional Purpose
- To assess student knowledge and understanding of unit topics

Materials and Handouts
- Preassessment (Handout 1A)
- Preassessment Answer Key (Teacher Resource 1)
- Eleven 1-inch cubes per student

Activities
1. Explain to students that they will be beginning a new unit of study focused on spatial reasoning. Tell students that in order to get a good sense of how much they already know and to be able to tell how much they have learned by the end of the unit, they will need to take a preassessment. Distribute the Preassessment (Handout 1A) and have students complete it individually, using the cubes when needed.

2. Collect and score the preassessments using the Preassessment Answer Key (Teacher Resource 1).

3. Have students discuss which aspects of the preassessment they found difficult. Explain that throughout the unit they will be thinking about challenging questions that relate to concepts on the preassessment.

Notes to Teacher
1. The preassessment given in this lesson serves multiple purposes. Performance on the preassessment should establish a baseline against which performance on the postassessment may be compared. In addition, teachers may use information obtained from preassessments to aid in instructional planning as strengths and areas for improvement among students become apparent.

2. Students should have a unit notebook or folder that they can use throughout the unit to respond to math journal questions, other written assignments, and to keep any handouts from the unit. The notebook also can hold a running list of unit vocabulary, which should be displayed in the classroom in chart form.

Assessment
- Preassessment

Preassessment (Handout 1A)

Directions: Do your best to answer the following questions.

1. Construct a building with cubes by placing the given number of cubes on each square.

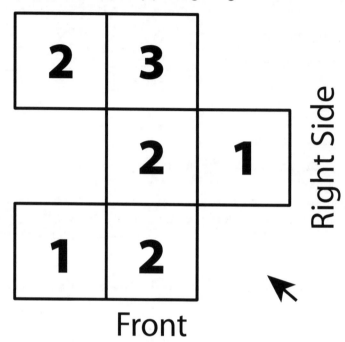

2. Draw a picture of the building as it looks from the corner marked with the arrow. You may use the dot paper below or the back of this page to draw your picture.

3. On the back of this page or a blank piece of paper, draw the following three views of the building in #1 above:

    a. the top view

    b. the front view

    c. the right side view

4. Give an example of each of the following:

    a. one-dimensional object _____

    b. two-dimensional object _____

    c. three-dimensional object _____

5. How many cubes are needed to build this building? Show your work.

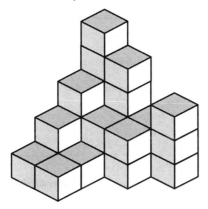

6. What is a fractal?

_____

_____

_____

7. A roll of wrapping paper is cut with a knife at the angle shown. If the paper is unwrapped, what does the shaded piece look like? Draw it.

8. Haley opened a can of jellied cranberries that came out of the can as a cylinder. She cut the cylinder on the dotted lines as shown. She took the shaded slice out and put it on a plate. Draw the shape of the slice.

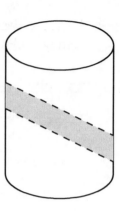

9. She opened another can of jellied cranberries and made one slice through points A, B, C, and D and put it on a plate. Draw the shape of the slice.

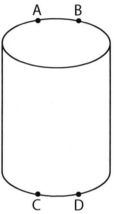

10. When she cut the third can, the knife passed through points A, B, and C in the diagram. Draw the shape of the cross section (the surface of the cranberries where the knife passed through).

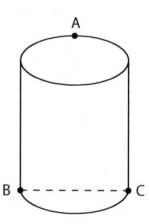

Extra Challenge Questions:

1. Imagine a building made with cubes that are placed as shown below in the diagram. Do not build the building.

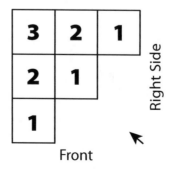

2. Draw a picture of the building as it looks from the corner marked with the arrow. You may use the dot paper below or the back of this page to draw your picture.

3. On the back of this page or on a blank piece of paper, draw the following three views of the building in #1 above:

   a. the top view

   b. the front view

   c. the right side view

Preassessment Answer Key
(Teacher Resource 1)

Directions: Do your best to answer the following questions.

1. Construct a building with cubes by placing the given number of cubes on each square.

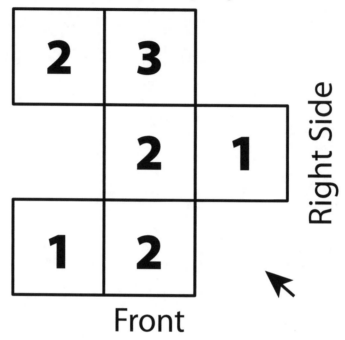

2. Draw a picture of the building as it looks from the corner marked with the arrow. You may use the dot paper below or the blank space to draw your picture.

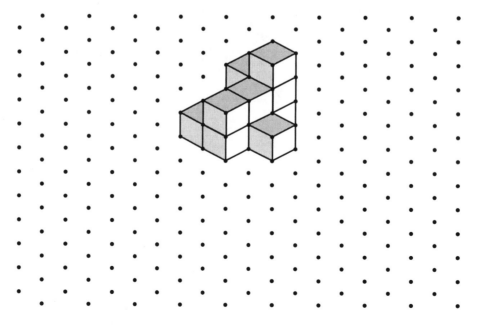

3. On the back of this page or on a blank piece of paper, draw the following three views of the building in #1 above:

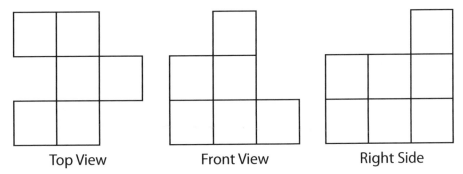

Top View   Front View   Right Side

4. Give an example of each of the following:
    a. one-dimensional object

    A line on a piece of paper or other similar example

    b. a two-dimensional object

    A rectangle drawn on a piece of paper, a picture of something, etc.

    c. a three-dimensional object

    A box of cereal, a pencil, or any object that can be picked up

5. How many cubes are needed to build this building? Show your work.

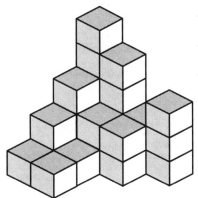

26; one way to find out is to count the number

of cubes in each tower, write the number on top of the

tower, and then add all of the numbers

6. What is a fractal?

A fractal is a geometric pattern that can be split into parts, each of which is

(at least approximately) a reduced-size copy of the whole.

7. A roll of wrapping paper is cut with a knife at the angle shown. If the paper is unwrapped, what does the shaded piece look like?

8. Haley opened a can of jellied cranberries that came out of the can as a cylinder. She cut the cylinder on the dotted lines as shown. She took the shaded slice out and put it on a plate. Draw the shape of the shaded slice as it looks on the plate.

It is an ellipse and can be drawn in any direction on the page.

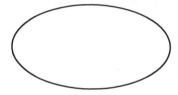

9. She opened another can of jellied cranberries and made one slice through points A, B, C, and D and put it on a plate. Draw the shape of the slice.

10. When she cut the third can, the knife passed through points A, B, and C in the diagram. Draw the shape of the cross section (the surface of the cranberries where the knife passed through).

Extra Challenge Questions:

1. Imagine a building made with cubes that are placed as shown below in the diagram. Do not build the building.

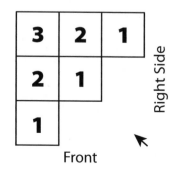

Front

Right Side

2. Draw a picture of the building as it looks from the corner marked with the arrow. You may use the dot paper below or the blank space to draw your picture.

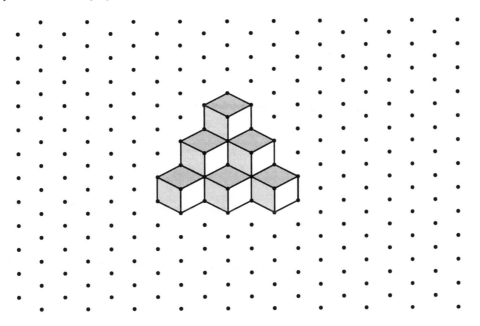

3. On the back of this page or a blank piece of paper, draw the following three views of the building in #1 above:

    a. the top view

    b. the front view

    c. the right side view

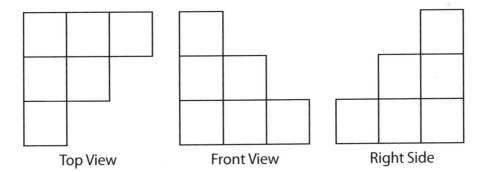

      Top View   Front View   Right Side

Lesson 2: Introduction to Dimensions

Instructional Purpose

- To introduce the idea of dimensions

Materials and Handouts

- Pop-Up Cubes (Handout 2A)
- Different Dimensions (Handout 2B)
- Different Dimensions Answer Key (Teacher Resource 1)
- Centimeter graph paper
- Scissors
- Ten 1-inch cubes per student
- *Flatland* by Edwin A. Abbott
- Piece of colored paper

Activities

1. Write the word *dimension* on the board. Have students discuss the meaning of the word in groups and then discuss as a whole class.

2. Draw a line segment on the board as an example of a one-dimensional object. Tell students that a set of points that is extended in one direction is called one-dimensional. Emphasize that you need only one measurement to determine the length of a one-dimensional object.

3. Define two-dimensional as a description of something that has both length and width; therefore, it requires two measurements. Give examples of two-dimensional objects such as rectangles, circles, and floor tiles.

4. Use the rolled-up overhead screen in the classroom as a model of a line segment. Tell students to imagine it to be a set of fat points lined up in one direction. Then pull the screen down and tell students that the screen now has a length and a width. Point out that the rectangle created requires two measurements to describe it—length and width—therefore it is two-dimensional.

5. Explain that three-dimensional objects have depth as well as length and width. Give examples of three-dimensional objects in the room such as furniture, people, and books. A box is a good model for a three-dimensional object as the length, width, and height can be seen clearly and measured.

6. Distribute Pop-Up Cubes (Handout 2A) and have students make the cubes using graph paper. Point out that three numbers are needed to give the size of this rectangular solid—length, width, and height. Tell students that an N-dimensional object is one that requires N numbers to describe a location on it.

7. Ask students how many dimensions a point has. (Zero; because it has no length, width, or depth.)

8. Tell students about the book, *Flatland* by Edwin A. Abbott, which is about a made-up two-dimensional world. Use the following questions to discuss the idea of Flatland. They may think of a tabletop as a model for Flatland; by stooping so your eye level is at the tabletop, you can see how inhabitants of Flatland view their world. Do not observe Flatland from above, as the third dimension does not exist for them!

9. Ask students the following questions:
    a. What do you think the inhabitants of Flatland look like? (Polygons, circles, line segments, or anything that is flat or lies in a plane)
    b. How do the inhabitants of Flatland move about their world? (Sliding around)
    c. Let's say a square meets a hexagon in Flatland. How does the hexagon look from the perspective of the square? (It looks like a segment.)
    d. If a square meets a line segment, how does it look to the square? (If the line segment is heading straight at the square, it will appear as a single point; if it is at an angle, it will appear as a line segment.)
    e. If a sphere falls into Flatland from another galaxy, what does the sphere look like to the inhabitants of Flatland? (A point, the point of contact. They cannot see the rest of it as the third dimension does not exist for them.)

10. Distribute Different Dimensions (Handout 2B) and have students complete it individually.

11. In their math journals or notebooks, have students write a paragraph about what the fourth dimension might be. Have students share their ideas. Offer them the opportunity to read about other peoples' ideas about the fourth dimension and report back.

Notes to Teacher

1. We represent a point with a dot so that we can see it, but it has no length, width, or height. Students may argue that a point has length and width that just happen to be small. However, you need to reinforce the idea that it is not the representation, but the definition that determines what a point is. It is a location in space, and has no dimensions.

2. Euclid, a Greek mathematician who lived from about 325 BC–265 BC and often is called the father of geometry, gave the vague definition of a point as "that which has no part."

3. It is difficult to say that any real-world object is one-dimensional because the width is greater than a point. Even a line drawn on paper has width greater than a point; however, we think of items such as spaghetti as being one-dimensional objects because the width is negligible. The distinction between two and three dimensions is the most relevant for functioning in the real world. Therefore, this unit will concentrate on two and three dimensions and movement between those dimensions.

4. *Flatland* was written as a satire on Victorian society and class distinctions; it was first published in the 1880s. Edwin A. Abbott described women as line segments and men were polygons whose importance was indicated by the number of sides. He made priests circles, thus giving them an infinite number of sides. You might

read the book yourself and decide which elements to use for discussion. You also can find summaries of the book on the Internet.

5. You might use these examples to illustrate dimensions for students in terms of mathematical conventions.
    a. A number line is one-dimensional. In order to know where a point is, you need to give only one number. For example, if a point is at 7, it is 7 units to the right of 0.
    b. A set of x-y coordinate axes represents a two-dimensional plane. In order to know where a point is, you need to give two numbers. For example, if a point is at (3,-2), it is 3 units to the right of the origin and then 2 units down. You may search "Cartesian coordinates in two dimensions" on the Internet for drawings.
    c. A set of x-y-z coordinate axes represents a three-dimensional plane. In order to know where a point is, you need to give three numbers. For example, if a point is at (4,1,-2), it is 4 units forward in the direction of the x-axis, then one unit in the direction of the y-axis, and then 2 units backwards in the direction of the z-axis. You may search "Cartesian coordinates in three dimensions" on the Internet for drawings.

Assessment

- Different Dimensions (Handout 2B)

Extensions

- Read *A Wrinkle in Time* by Madeleine L'Engle. Discuss how dimensions are important in the story.
- Click on "Multidimensional Math" and "Imagining Other Dimensions" for a demonstration of one, two, three, and four dimensions at http://www.pbs.org/wgbh/nova/elegant.
- Read Dr. Math's response at The Math Forum @ Drexel on the subject of "Beyond the Third Dimension" at http://mathforum.org/library/drmath/view/57230.html.

Pop-Up Cubes (Handout 2A)

Directions: Use the following procedures to make models of cubes.

1. You will need one piece of colored paper and one piece of centimeter graph paper for each student. (Commercial graph paper with grid lines on both sides is best.)

2. Have students fold both papers in half horizontally ("hamburger" style).

3. Using the graph paper, make a cut with scissors one unit in from the fold, move over one unit, and cut in one unit again.

4. Fold the flap back and forth so that it has a sharp crease at its hinge.

5. Open the paper and push the flap out on the side of the paper that is inside the fold; one cubic centimeter should pop up.

6. To make another cube that is 2 x 2 x 2: Return to the folded graph paper. Move over one block from the cubic unit, and make a 2 x 2 cut.

7. Repeat steps 4 and 5.

8. Continue this process until you have five cubes so that the length of the edge is increased by one unit each time.

9. Each of the cuts should "pop up" so that you have a row of cubes that are increasing in size.

10. Place the colored sheet of paper behind the graph paper to provide contrast and increase the 3-D look of the models. See the graphic below for an idea of what the pop-up cubes should look like.

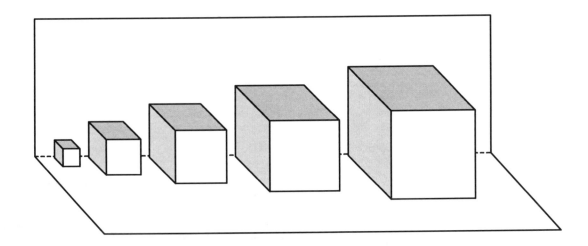

Name:_____ Date:_____

Different Dimensions (Handout 2B)

Directions: Use the information below to fill in the chart.

The following points are inhabitants of various "planets."   P   Q   R
●   ●   ●

Number of dimensions that can be experienced on the planet.	Draw or describe the planet.	Describe how the points are able to move within the planet.
1-D		
2-D		
3-D		

Different Dimensions Answer Key (Teacher Resource 1)

Directions: Use the information below to fill in the chart.

The following points are inhabitants of various "planets."   P   Q   R
●   ●   ●

Number of dimensions that can be experienced on the planet.	Draw or describe the planet.	Describe how the points are able to move within the planet.
1-D	It is a line or a curved path.	They slide backwards and forwards on the line only. They cannot "jump" over each other.
2-D	It is some kind of flat surface.	They may slide in any direction on the flat surface but may not "jump" over each other.
3-D	It has an open space.	The points can slide or "jump" in any direction.

Lesson 3: Drawing Cube Structures

Instructional Purpose

- To represent three-dimensional objects in two dimensions
- To use two-dimensional representations to build three-dimensional structures

Materials and Handouts

- Drawing Example (Handout 3A)
- Drawing Cube Structures (Handout 3B)
- Drawing Cube Structures Answer Key (Teacher Resource 1)
- Rotating Figures (Handout 3C)
- Rotating Figures Answer Key (Teacher Resource 2)
- Thirty multilink cubes per group
- Five 1-inch cubes per student
- Centimeter grid paper
- Isometric dot paper
- Math journals

Activities

1. Have students put a cube on their desk and draw a picture of it in their math journal. Encourage students to share their pictures and discuss the difficulty of capturing the three-dimensional perspective on a two-dimensional surface.

2. Distribute isometric dot paper and demonstrate how to draw a cube. Use a transparency of the isometric dot paper and follow the directions below (see Figure 1).

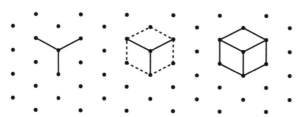

Figure 1. How to draw a cube.

   a. Draw a Y shape as shown.
   b. Draw a hexagon around the Y.
   c. Distribute centimeter grid paper and demonstrate how to draw a cube. Use a transparency of the centimeter grid paper and follow the directions below (see Figure 2).
   d. Draw a square that is two units on a side.
   e. Draw three segments that are diagonals of a unit square as shown in Figure 2.
   f. Complete the picture with the last two segments.

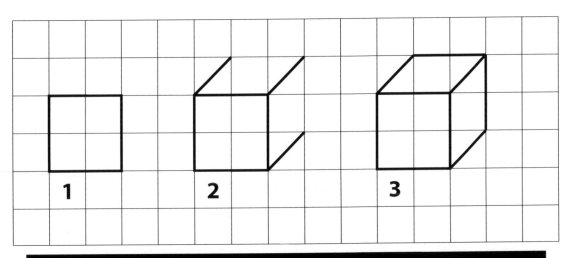

Figure 2. Drawing a cube on centimeter paper.

    g. Discuss with students the similarities and differences using centimeter grid paper and isometric dot paper. Point out that in this lesson we do not want to draw the figure by viewing it directly from above, front, or side because the picture would not reveal enough detail and would not give the impression of a three-dimensional object. Distribute Drawing Example (Handout 3A) and display as a transparency.

3. Distribute Drawing Cube Structures (Handout 3B) and have students complete it. Point out to students that when they make the drawing on the rectangular grid paper, they should rotate the original figure 45 degrees counterclockwise. If they have trouble, they should build the figure with cubes.

4. Distribute Rotating Figures (Handout 3C) and have students complete it. Have students glue three wooden cubes together as shown in the handout and save the cubes for a future lesson.

5. Make transparencies of the student drawings in Drawing Cube Structures (Handout 3B). Place one of the transparencies on the overhead projector and turn it on for 5 seconds. Turn off the overhead projector and have students build the structure using 1-inch cubes. Turn on the projector for students to check their buildings.

Notes to Teacher

1. The interactive math site http://illuminations.nctm.org/tools/isometric/isometric. asp#ft can be used to create dynamic drawings on isometric dot paper using edges, faces, or cubes. Students can shift, rotate, color, decompose, and view figures in 3-D or 2-D using this site.

2. Grid paper and isometric dot paper can be found online by using the search terms "grid paper" or "isometric dot paper."

3. Cubes for lessons can be located at http://www.etacuisenaire.com, using the search term "cubes" or check http://www.minimathprojects.com and click on "Order Form" to find packages of 108 1-inch cubes.

Assessment

- Drawing Cube Structures (Handout 3B)
- Rotating Figures (Handout 3C)

Extensions

1. Make the following cube structure (see Figure 3) using four cubes.

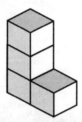

a. How many different views can be drawn for this figure? (24)
b. Draw all possible views on isometric dot paper.
c. Explain why there are so many more views of this structure versus the one you drew in Drawing Cube Structures (Handout 3B).

2. Use four multilink (snap-together) cubes to make various cube structures. Repeat the drawing exercise from Handout 3B with these structures. Classify them by the number of ways you can draw views on isometric dot paper. Ask students these questions:
a. What numbers of distinct views are possible?
b. What patterns do you notice?
c. Can you predict how many different views are possible for a given cube structure?

Drawing Example (Handout 3A)

Directions: Use this example to help you draw structures properly.

Draw the figure at a 45-degree angle (a vertical edge is in the front, not a face).	Do not draw the figure straightforward like the one below (if you look directly at the front, you don't see the depth of the structure).

Drawing Cube Structures (Handout 3B)

Directions: Follow the procedures listed below.

1.   Copy the following drawing onto the isometric dot paper to the right of the drawing.

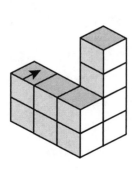

2.   Draw the same figure on the rectangular grid of dots below.

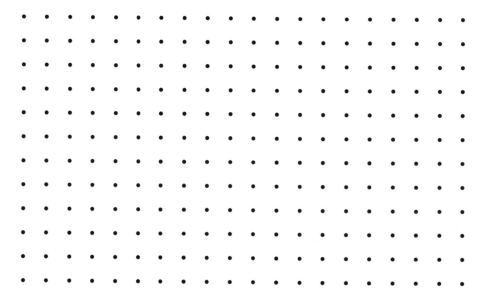

3. a) Build the structure pictured below using four cubes. Rotate it clockwise 90 degrees (so that the tower is in the back).

4. a) Build another cube structure of your choice using five cubes.

3. b) Draw the new view of the figure.

4. b) Draw your structure here.

3. c) Draw it here, too.

4. c) Draw it here, too.

Drawing Cube Structures Answer Key (Teacher Resource 1)

Directions: Follow the procedures listed below.

1. Copy the following drawing onto the isometric dot paper to the right of the drawing.

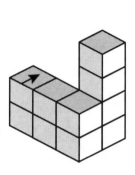

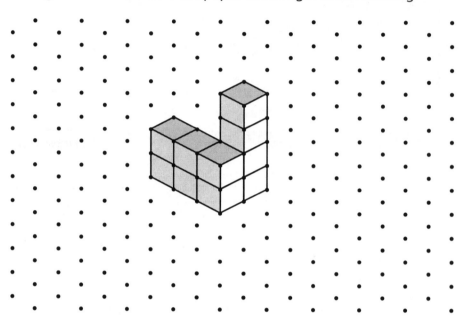

2. Draw the same figure on the rectangular grid of dots below.

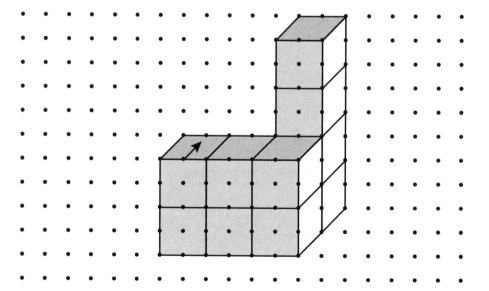

3. a) Build the structure pictured below using four cubes. Rotate it clockwise 90 degrees (so that the tower is in the back).

4. a) Build another cube structure of your choice using five cubes.

3. b) Draw the new view of the figure.

4. b) Draw your structure here.

3. c) Draw it here, too.

4. c) Draw it here, too.

Name:_____ Date:_____

Rotating Figures (Handout 3C)

Directions: Rotate this figure and draw it in as many other orientations as you can. How many different pictures are possible?

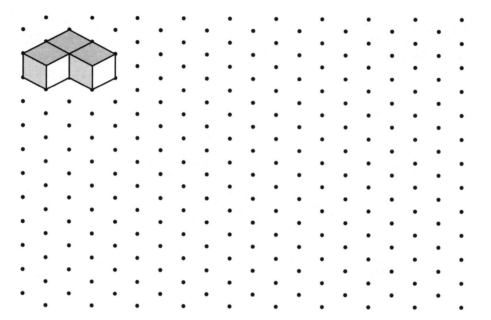

Rotating Figures Answer Key (Teacher Resource 2)

Directions: Rotate this figure and draw it in as many other orientations as you can. How many different pictures are possible?

These are the 12 rotations of the figure:

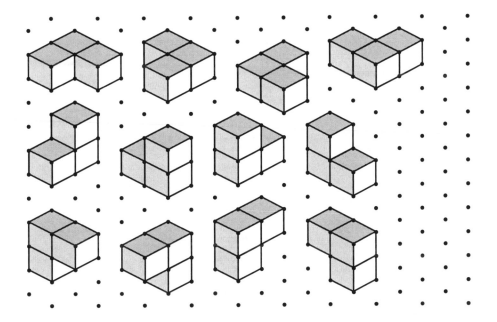

Lesson 4: Projecting Solids Into Two Dimensions

Instructional Purpose

- To project three-dimensional objects into two dimensions
- To record the projection using a mat plan

Materials and Handouts

- Mat Plan Example (Handout 4A)
- Mat Plans (Handout 4B)
- Mat Plans Answer Key (Teacher Resource 1)
- Different Views (Handout 4C)
- Different Views Answer Key (Teacher Resource 2)
- Set of wooden geometric solids
- Objects for projecting (e.g., JELL-O box, coffee mug, black binder clip, soup can, penny, spool of thread, stapler, tape dispenser, apple)
- Math journals

Activities

Part I

1. Tape newspaper to the front of the overhead projector so that students cannot see what you are setting on the glass. Put a clean transparency sheet on the glass to protect it. Show students a rectangular prism (with the length, width, and height of all different measurements, such as a chalk box) by setting it on the center of the projector glass. Tell students that this is the top view. Turn it to its side and tell students that this is the side view. Turn it so it rests on the front and tell students that this is the front view. Ask students to identify the object.

2. Tell students that the shadow or image of the solid on the screen is called a projection because you are projecting the image. Explain that they are looking at a two-dimensional image of a three-dimensional object. Ask students how many different projections there are for a given object. (Three, there is a projection for each dimension. Use the top view, side view, and front view to identify the three views.)

3. Put a hemisphere, from a set of geometric solids, on the overhead projector sitting it on its circular base. Ask students to identify what possible geometric solids it might be. (Sphere, cylinder, cone, and hemisphere) Show students the side view and have them predict the front view. Show students the front view (which in this case is the same as the side view).

4. Repeat with a cone and pyramid. If you use a sphere, turn off the overhead projector and put a small piece of double-sided tape on the sphere. Tape it to the transparency so it does not roll. Then turn on the overhead.

5. Project some everyday objects on the overhead. Ask students how many views they need to see before they can identify the object. (Sometimes you might know

in two projections because the third view is the same as one of the others. For example, a cylinder has the same front view and side view.)

6. Put an object such as a book on the overhead. Show one view and ask students to identify the object. Share a second view, and then a third. Students may not know for sure that it is a book, but they should know it has the shape of a rectangular prism.

7. As with the sphere, turn off the overhead. Put a small piece of double-sided tape on the barrel of the mug on the opposite side of the handle. When you stick it to the transparency, the handle should be aimed upward and therefore not visible in the projection, as shown in Figure 4.

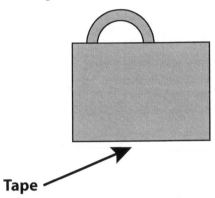

Tape

Figure 4. First orientation of the coffee cup.

8. Turn on the overhead. Tell students that this is the side view and ask what the object might be. Students will not know as the projection should be similar to a rectangle. Turn the mug on its side so students can see the front view that looks something like Figure 5.

Figure 5. Second orientation of coffee cup.

9. Have students draw what they think the top view looks like in their math journal or notebook. It should be something like Figure 6.

Figure 6. Top view of coffee cup.

35

10. Check by putting the mug on the overhead projector or have students stand over the cup and look directly down into it. Hint: If you cover one eye you get a flatter image.

11. Project other objects such as a JELL-O box, binder clip, soup can, square-based box, pencil, square pyramid, cube, and sphere. Have students classify the objects according to their projections using the following categories:
    a. All three views different (JELL-O box, binder clip)
    b. Two views the same (soup can, square-based box, pencil, square pyramid)
    c. All three views the same (cube and sphere)

12. Have students build cube structures and draw projections on grid paper: top view, front view, and side view. Encourage students to look directly at the structure with one eye covered or closed. This takes away the depth perception and makes the image look two-dimensional. Ask students what can be gained by seeing all three projections.

13. Give students a mat plan (you can copy one from this book or make your own). Ask them to draw the front view, top view, and side view without actually building the structure with cubes.

14. Discuss that these two-dimensional images of three-dimensional objects are created by projecting top, front, and side views called *orthogonal projections* in mathematics. Have students look for the term *orthogonal* in a dictionary and report on their findings.

15. Tell students that shadows are projections. If you can darken the room enough to make a clear shadow, use a good flashlight and hold it about 4 to 5 feet away from an object and view the shadow on the wall. Shine the light from the top, side, and front views of the object. The effect is similar to that of using an overhead projector to project shadows.

Part II
1. Distribute Mat Plan Example (Handout 4A) and display a transparency. Ask students how many cubes are needed to build the structure and how they know (12). Tell students that one way to record information about structures they build is to make a mat plan. A mat plan is a floor plan of the base of the structure with the number of cubes placed on each square of the plan. Ask student to compare the mat plan to the top view projection of an object. (The same in shape but the projection has no numbers written on it.)

2. Distribute Mat Plans (Handout 4B) and have students complete the handout. Tell students if they build the structure as shown, they should rotate it 45 degrees to arrive at the traditional orientation for the mat plan.

3. Have students work in pairs with a divider between them so they cannot see their partner's structure. Have one student build a cube structure and keep it hidden from his or her partner. Have the student create a mat plan for the structure and pass the mat plan to his or her partner. The partner should build the structure following the mat plan. Remove the barrier to compare the structures.

4. Distribute Different Views (Handout 4C) and have students complete it. For extra challenge, have them complete it without using cubes.

5. Encourage students to bring in objects to project on the overhead projector. This will prompt them to look at everyday objects with respect to the nature of their projections. They can use a flashlight at home to try various projections.

Notes to Teacher

1. If you have a glass table at home, you can practice projections by placing objects on the table and viewing them from underneath. You may suggest this activity to students to try if they have a glass-topped table at home.

2. The projection of the right side view of a cube structure often is different from the projection of the left side view. If the directions say, "Side view," it means "Right side view."

Assessment

- Mat Plans (Handout 4B)
- Different Views (Handout 4C)

Extensions

1. Go to this Web site (http://www.learner.org/teacherslab/math/geometry/space/plotplan/index.html) and see if you can make a mat plan that is correct for the given front and right side projections. This Web site uses the term *plot plan* instead of mat plan.

2. Play the game Point Out the View, in which characters positioned around a cube structure need to show what the structure looks like to them. The game can be found at http://pbskids.org/cyberchase/games/pointofview/pointofview.html.

3. Describe in your math journal what a projection from two dimensions to one dimension would look like. Hint: Think of a flashlight in Flatland shining from above the triangle in Figure 7 and projecting a shadow onto the x-axis. The shadow is one-dimensional because it only has length.

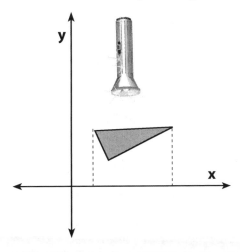

Figure 7. Flashlight projection above triangle.

4. Then repeat by shining the light from the right of this triangle (see Figure 8) and projecting a shadow onto the y-axis. The shadow is one-dimensional because it only has length.

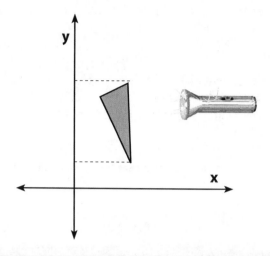

Figure 8. Flashlight projection to side of triangle.

5. Use activities from pages 41–51 from the book *Spatial Problem Solving With Cuisenaire Rods*. This set of blackline masters has a challenging section on making drawings (top, front, side views) of structures made from Cuisenaire Rods.

6. Explore http://www.fi.uu.nl/toepassingen/00200/toepassing_wisweb.en.html, which is a three-dimensional object viewer. It shows a drawing of a three-dimensional objects in four different views: front, left, right, and top. Choose some objects to view and then draw the views before the applet shows them.

7. Create a set of projections for a cube structure such that there is more than one solution (i.e., more than one structure has these projections). Give the mat plan of your multiple solutions.

Resources

- *Connected Mathematics: Ruins of Montarek* by Glenda Lappan: This unit from the Connected Mathematics project at Michigan State University does many of the projection type of problems done in this lesson. It involves creating and interpreting architectural and isometric representations.
- *Spatial Problem Solving With Cuisenaire Rods* by Patricia S. Davidson and Robert E. Willcutt: This set of blackline masters has a challenging section on making drawings (top, front, side views) of structures made from Cuisenaire Rods.
- "Developing Spatial Sense: Comparing Appearance to Reality" by Gwen Kelly, Tim Ewers, and Lanna Proctor in *The Mathematics Teacher*, December 2002, pp. 702–712: This article has eight pages containing 16 task cards involving various top, front, and side view activities.
- *Spatial Visualization Unit* (Middle Grades Math Project), by Mary Jean Winter, Glenda Lappan, Elizabeth Phillips, and William Fitzgerald: This is an extensive unit that deals with isometric drawings and mat plans.

Mat Plan Example (Handout 4A)

Directions: Use the structure's image below to help you visualize how mat plans show how many cubes are in each tower of a structure. The figure at the top is the view of the cube structure as it looks from the corner marked with the arrow in the bottom figure.

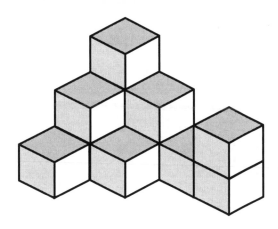

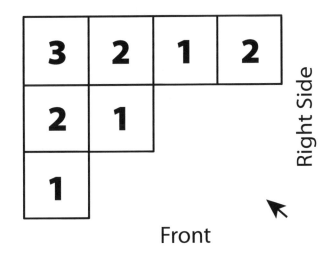

Right Side

Front

Mat Plans (Handout 4B)

Directions: How many cubes does it take to build each of these? Make a mat plan for each structure.

	Guess:	Make a mat plan:
	Build and Check:	
	Guess:	Make a mat plan:
	Build and Check:	

	Guess:	Make a mat plan:
	Build and check:	
	Guess:	Make a mat plan:
	Build and check:	

Mat Plans Answer Key
(Teacher Resource 1)

Directions: How many cubes does it take to build each of these? Make a mat plan for each structure.

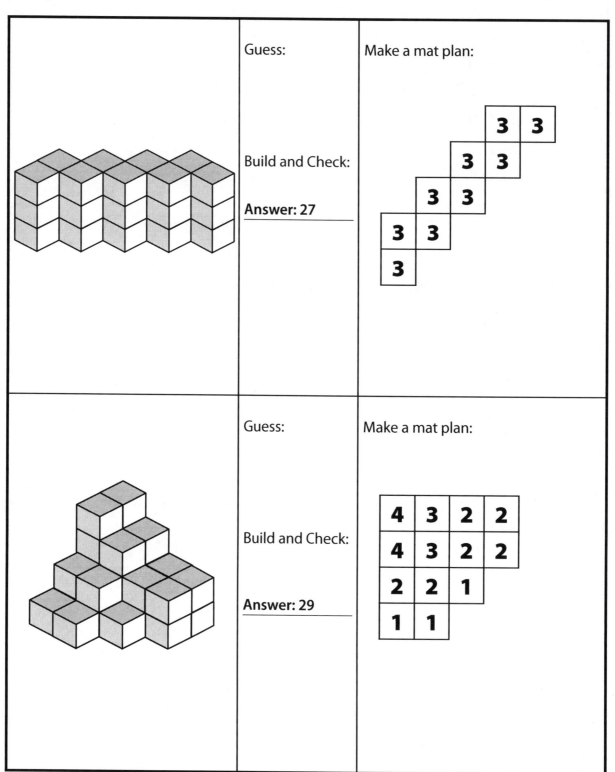

Guess:

Build and Check:

Answer: 27

Make a mat plan:

			3	3
		3	3	
	3	3		
3	3			
3				

Guess:

Build and Check:

Answer: 29

Make a mat plan:

4	3	2	2
4	3	2	2
2	2	1	
1	1		

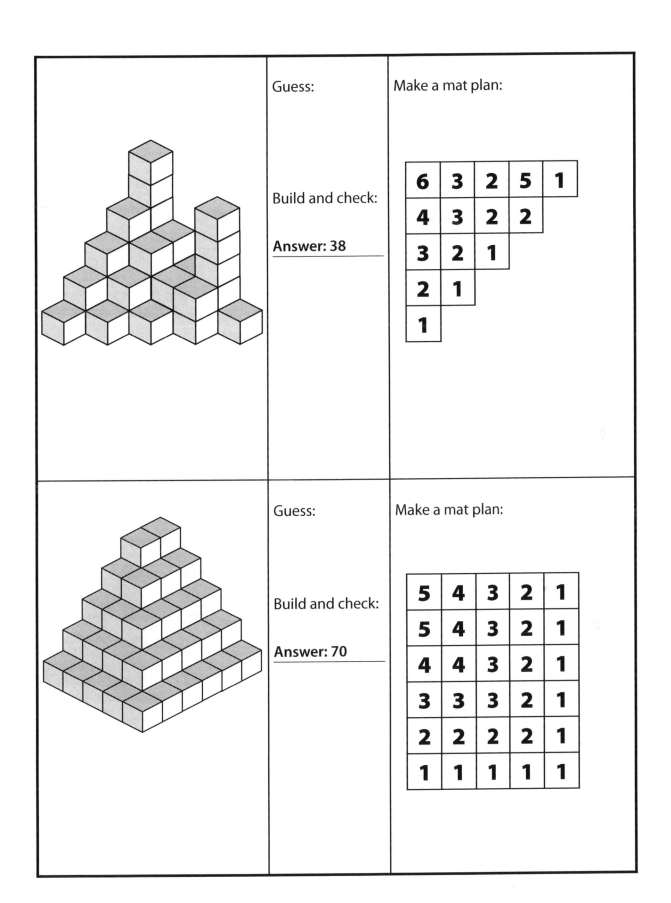

Guess:

Build and check:

Answer: 38

Make a mat plan:

6	3	2	5	1
4	3	2	2	
3	2	1		
2	1			
1				

Guess:

Build and check:

Answer: 70

Make a mat plan:

5	4	3	2	1
5	4	3	2	1
4	4	3	2	1
3	3	3	2	1
2	2	2	2	1
1	1	1	1	1

Different Views (Handout 4C)

Directions: Use each mat plan to construct a building. Draw the top view, front view, and right side view.

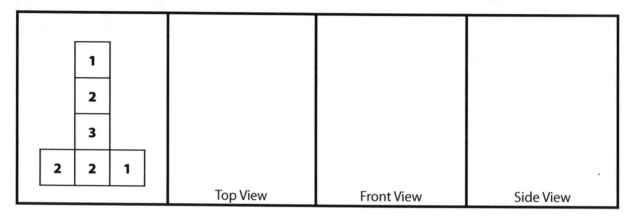

| | Top View | Front View | Side View |

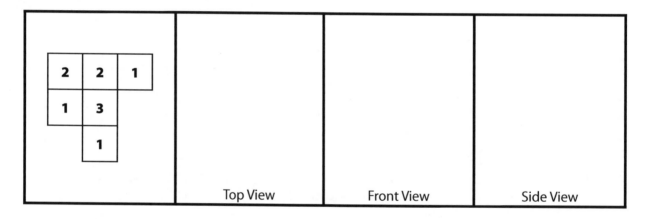

| | Top View | Front View | Side View |

| | Top View | Front View | Side View |

Directions: Build the cube structure from the three projections given. Make a mat plan for your structure.

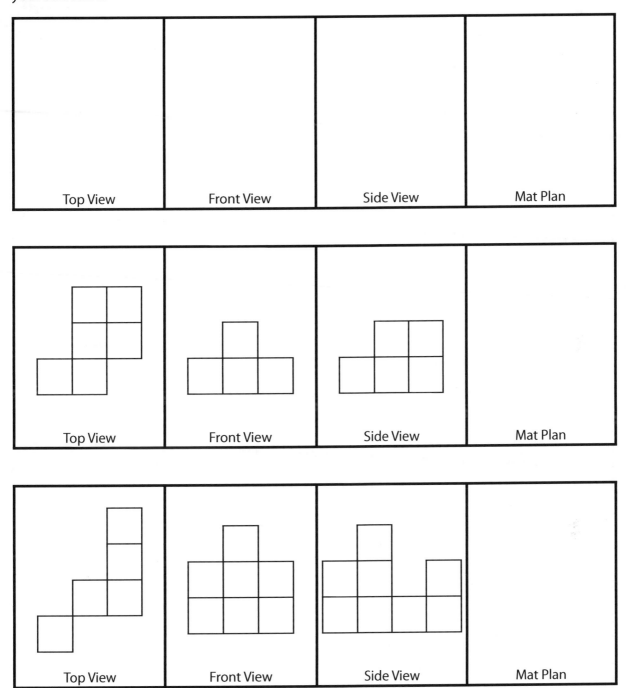

Different Views Answer Key
(Teacher Resource 2)

Directions: Use each mat plan to construct a building. Draw the top view, front view, and right side view.

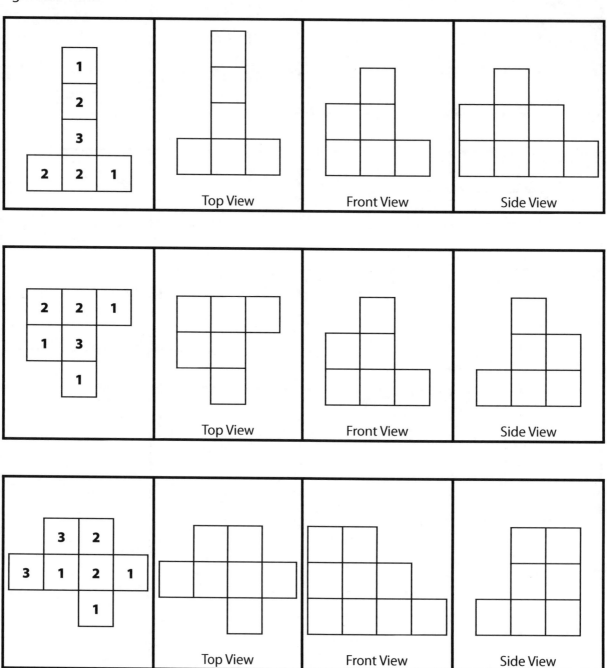

Top View Front View Side View

Top View Front View Side View

Top View Front View Side View

Directions: Build the cube structure from the three projections given. Make a mat plan for your structure.

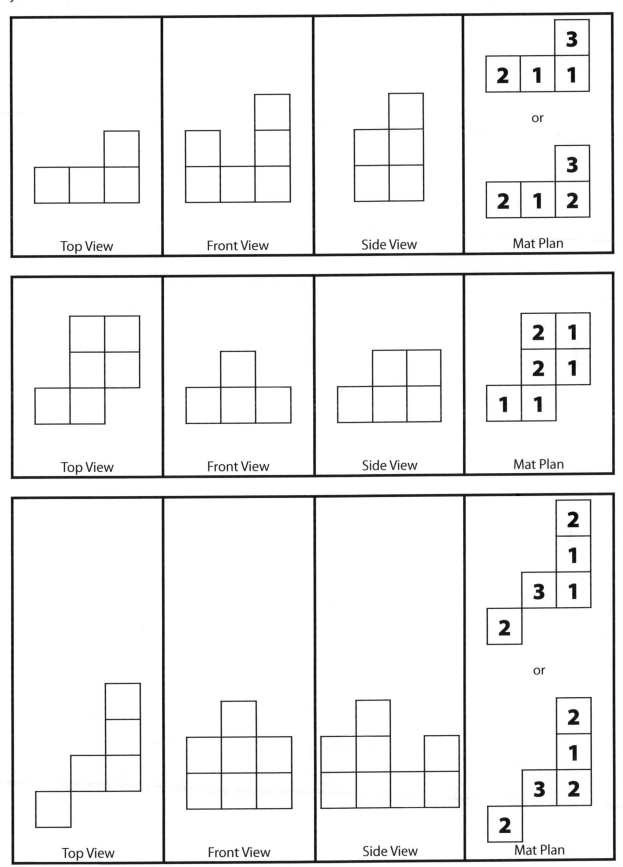

Top View   Front View   Side View   Mat Plan

Lesson 5: Polycubes

Instructional Purpose

- To observe the patterns made by combining cubes to form structures

Materials and Handouts

- Sample Soma Solution (Handout 5A)
- Soma Recording Sheet (Handout 5B)
- Soma Practice (Handout 5C)
- Five Cubes (Teacher Resource 1)
- Twenty-seven 1-inch cubes per student
- Glue (not glue sticks)
- Permanent markers
- Gallon-size zipper bags

Activities

1. Give each student a gallon-size zipper bag and 27 one-inch cubes. Have students build all the nonrectangular solids possible using three cubes joined at the faces. Remind students that if they rotate or flip a solid and it matches the original then it is considered the same structure for this challenge. Ask students how many answers they found. (One; see Figure 9)

Figure 9. Only possible nonrectangular solid with three cubes.

2. Have students make all the nonrectangular solids possible using four cubes. Ask students how many answers they found. (Six; see Figure 10)

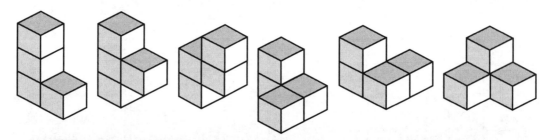

Figure 10. The six possible nonrectangular solids using four cubes.

3. Number the seven pieces in the following order on a transparency (see Figure 11) using a permanent marker. Label every exposed square with the number assigned to the piece. Tell students to be careful with pieces five and six because they are mirror images of each other, not just a rotation.

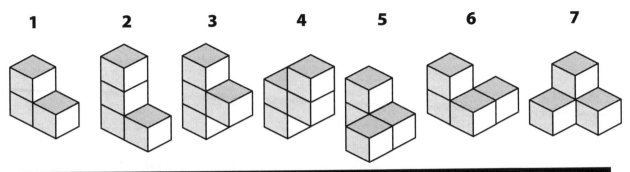

1   2   3   4   5   6   7

Figure 11. Labels for the seven nonrectangular solids found using three and four cubes.

4. You gave the students 27 cubes. Ask students why the number 27 is special. (It is a perfect cube, meaning 3^3.) Ask students why the word *cube* is used to describe a third power. Explain that a rectangular prism with the same three dimensions (length, width, and height) is a cube.

5. Challenge students to form a 3 x 3 x 3 cube using all seven nonrectangular polycubes formed above. Tell students there are 240 distinctive ways to do it (see Figure 12 for one way). This puzzle is called a Soma Cube.

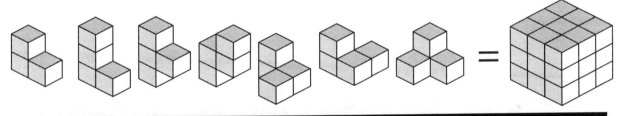

Figure 12. One possible Soma solution.

6. Give students background information about the Soma cube. Explain that Piet Hein conceived the idea in 1936 in Denmark, during a lecture about quantum physics. The speaker talked about a room divided by cubes, inspiring Piet Hein to imagine this geometric theory: If you take all irregular shapes that can be formed by combining no more than four cubes all the same size and joined at their faces, these shapes can be combined to form a larger cube. When the lecture was over, he glued 27 cubes together to form the 7 shapes and found that they could be combined to make a 3 x 3 x 3 cube. He called his set of figures Soma.

7. Distribute Sample Soma Solution (Handout 5A) and display it on the overhead projector. Tell students that this is one solution to the cube. If they think of each of the layers of the cube as floors of a building, the solution sheet is a recording of the "blueprint" of each floor. Have students build the cube from these "blueprints."

8. Distribute the Soma Recording Sheet (Handout 5B). Have students find another solution to the cube and record it on the handout. Explain that the trick to this problem is to take a three-dimensional object and record its map in two dimensions. Encourage students to find as many solutions as they can.

9. Distribute Soma Practice (Handout 5C) and have students complete it. Have students record their solutions by writing the numbers of the pieces on the drawings.

10. Have students draw each of the Soma pieces on a separate piece of isometric or centimeter grid paper. They should draw as many different views of each piece as they can. Ask students: What patterns do you notice? Why can you draw more for some than others? (Rotating Figures Answer Key (Teacher Resource 2) shows the 12 ways to draw piece #1. There are 24 ways to draw piece #2, 8 ways to draw piece #7, and 12 ways to draw all of the other pieces.)

Notes to Teacher

1. Make a bulletin board for collecting Soma solutions. If a student finds a new solution, record it on a copy of the Soma Recording Sheet and post it on the bulletin board with the student's name. See how many solutions you can collect over the course of a semester. Have students suggest ways to determine if a solution is new to the collection or not.

2. Two sources for purchasing cubes are http://www.minimathprojects.com and http://www.etacuisenaire.com.

Assessment

- Have students find Soma solutions and record them in their math journals or notebooks. Require the number of different solutions appropriate for your students.
- Evaluate student drawings of the Soma pieces.

Extensions

1. Make and use isometric dot paper to draw the 29 pieces made from five multilink cubes. See Five Cubes (Teacher Resource 1) for the answers.

2. Build a new figure with your Soma pieces, draw the figure on isometric dot paper, and make an answer key on a copy of your drawing.

3. Make a mat plan for each of the seven Soma pieces.

4. Find the volume and surface area of each of the seven Soma pieces. Write a summary of your findings.

5. Find the volume and surface area of each of the figures in Soma Practice (Handout 5C).

Resources

- "Developing Spatial Skills With Three-Dimensional Puzzles," by John Izard, *The Arithmetic Teacher*, February 1990, pp. 44–47. This article gives a set of puzzle tasks that use Soma pieces.
- "Polycubes," by William J. Masalski, *The Mathematics Teacher*, January 1977, pp. 46–50. This article describes the Soma cube idea. It claims there are 1,105,920 ways to make the Soma cube. (This counts all rotations of the cube and flips of individual pieces as different solutions.) There are distinctly 240 different ways to make the cube.

Sample Soma Solution (Handout 5A)

Directions: This page contains one possible Soma solution. The numbers in the grid correspond to the numbered figures as demonstrated by your teacher.

5	5	2
5	6	2
6	6	2

Bottom Layer

7	4	2
5	4	4
6	3	4

Middle Layer

7	7	1
7	1	1
3	3	3

Top Layer

Soma Recording Sheet (Handout 5B)

Directions: Use these blank grids to record your own solutions to the Soma problem.

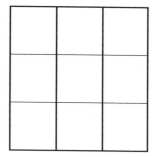

Bottom Layer

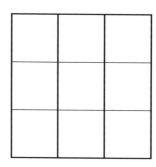

Bottom Layer

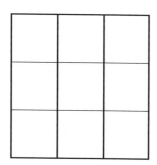

Middle Layer

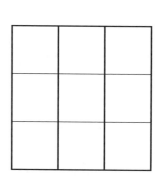

Middle Layer

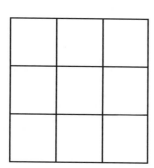

Top Layer

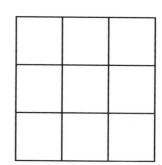

Top Layer

Soma Practice (Handout 5C)

Directions: Can you make these structures using all seven Soma pieces?
Mark the pictures with the numbers of your Soma pieces to show your solutions.

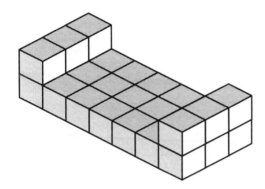

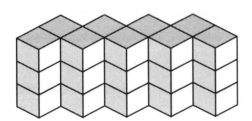

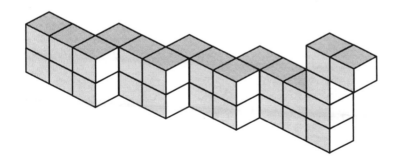

Five Cubes (Teacher Resource 1)

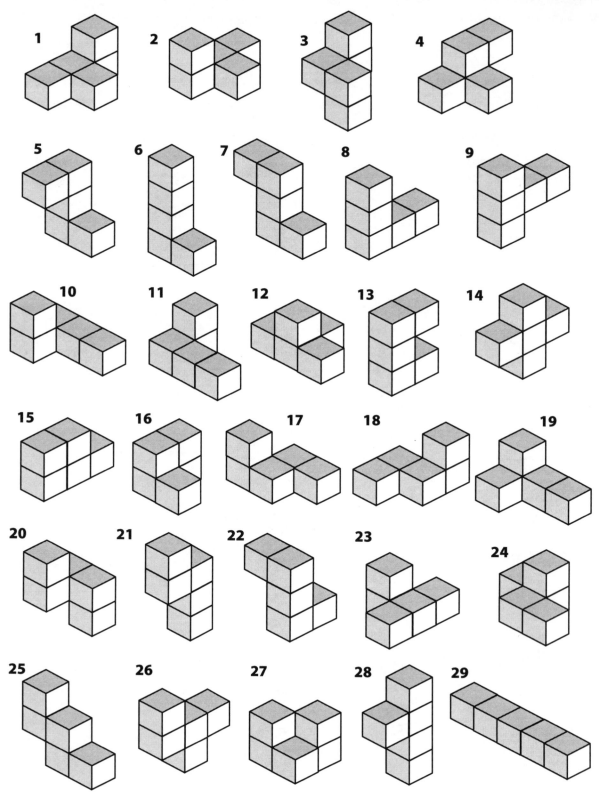

Lesson 6: Slices

Instructional Purpose

- To examine a sequence of two-dimensional slices of a three-dimensional object

Materials and Handouts

- Making Slices (Handout 6A)
- Slice the Apple (Handout 6B)
- Build the Mystery Solid (Handout 6C)
- Wrap and Slice (Handout 6D)
- Playdough or clay
- Fishing line or dental floss
- Items to slice, such as hardboiled eggs, bread, hot dogs, etc.
- Egg slicer (optional)
- Tissue paper

Activities

1. Do a demonstration for students of how three-dimensional objects can be divided into slices. For example, use an egg slicer to slice a hardboiled egg. Display the slices on the overhead projector.

2. Tell students that they will be dividing some solid objects into slices. Give them playdough and dental floss for cutting. Demonstrate how to make the cuts. Distribute Making Slices (Handout 6A) and have students work in groups to complete the first problem.

3. Have students share their drawings. Compare and contrast the drawings of the slices. (Some examples include: the five slices in the same direction are congruent; the slices are congruent to the exterior face that is parallel to the cuts; the rectangles resulting from the three directions of cuts are different from each other in dimensions but are all rectangular pieces.) Have students compare their slices to the image of the rectangular prism when it is placed on the overhead projector. (They should be the same.)

4. Have students work in groups to draw the slices of the cone in the second problem on Handout 6A. Debrief their answers as a whole class. Ask students how their slices are different from the slices in the first question. (Slices made in the same direction are similar in shape but not in size in cones. In the rectangular prism, however, all slices have the same shape and size.)

5. Distribute Slice the Apple (Handout 6B) and repeat the slicing exercise. Use three apples that you have bitten or cut pieces from the apples. Have students draw predictions of what the cross sections will look like, then cut the apple and compare the results.

6. Distribute Build the Mystery Solid (Handout 6C). Tell students that now they are going to reverse the process by looking at the cross sections first and then visualizing the solid. Have students work in groups to talk about the solid and build it out of playdough. Discuss their answers. (It should be a pyramid with a base that is an equilateral triangle, as shown in Figure 13. The height of the pyramid should be the same as the length of the edge of the triangle that forms the base.)

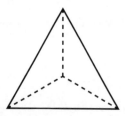

Figure 13. Pyramid with equilateral triangle base.

7. Explain that an MRI (magnetic resonance imaging) is like a set of x-rays of a body part. Tell students that it is a set of two-dimensional images that capture images of many parallel slices of tissue. A doctor who looks at the set of slides must process the images in his or her brain to identify the three-dimensional image. Tell students that you will model this kind of process with an object in a shoebox. Put a blob of clay or attach a solid somewhere in a shoebox. Draw the cross sections and challenge students to describe what the solid in the shoebox looks like and where it is positioned. As a follow-up activity, you might challenge students to place their own mystery object in a box and draw the cross sections for another student to "decode."

8. Distribute Wrap and Slice (Handout 6D) and have students complete it. Give students tissue paper. Discuss the activity with students.

Note to Teacher

1. Here is a teacher-tested and recommended playdough recipe:
   a. Mix together in a pan:
      i. ¾ cup salt
      ii. 3 cups flour
      iii. 6 teaspoons cream of tartar
      iv. 3 cups water
      v. 3 tablespoons vegetable oil
      vi. Food coloring

   b. Cook over medium heat, stirring constantly until the mixture is thick. It will pull away from the side of the pan when done. Store at room temperature in airtight containers.

Assessment

- Making Slices (Handout 6A)
- Slice the Apple (Handout 6B)

Extensions

1. Have students make a contour map, a two-dimensional representation of a three-dimensional landmass, using the following steps.
   a. Tell students to make a landform with clay and place it in a clear plastic box, such as a plastic shoebox-size storage box. Encourage students to make more than one hill. You might take digital photos of each box.
   b. Have students measure ½-inch increments on the side of the storage box from bottom to top. Tell them to mark these with lines made with a grease pencil or marker that shows up well on plastic.
   c. Have students pour water into the box to reach the level of the first ½-inch marking. Tell them to stretch plastic wrap tightly over the top of the box. Looking from above, they should gently trace the outline of the water-clay interface on the plastic wrap covering with a fine-tipped marker.
   d. Have students lift a corner of the plastic to allow a small place for water to be added. Add water to reach the level of the second ½-inch marking; repeat the tracing step.
   e. Have students repeat this process until the top of the landform is covered with water.
   f. Give students tissue or tracing paper and have them trace the map onto paper or copy the map on a copy machine. Tell them to label each of the lines according to the depth of the water.
   g. Have students exchange maps and build each other's landform from clay. Have students compare their constructions to the original model or the digital photos.

2. Have students devise and carry out a plan to find the volume in a lemon in cm³ by slicing it. Before students slice the lemon, have another student find the volume by submerging the lemon in a graduated cylinder to find the displacement of water. Have that student record the displacement in milliliters. Tell students that 1 ml = 1 cm³, and they can check the volume by the slicing method. Tell students that in calculus an analytical method for determining the volume of a solid uses an infinite number of slices to find the infinite sum.

3. Tell students to imagine that a cylindrical tank is half full of water and that we want to pump the water out of the top by pumping layers off the top of the surface of the water. Have students describe the shape of these layers if:
   a. the tank sits on its circular base (see Figure 14)
   b. the tank lays on its side (see Figure 15)

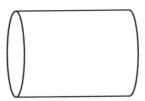

Figure 14. Tank sitting on its circular base.   **Figure 15.** Tank lying on its side.

4. Have students use a clear jar and fill it halfway with water to observe if they are having trouble.

5. Use a set of hollow plastic geometric models that have holes for filling them with water. Put water in various solids and have students tip until different polygonal shapes form at the surface of the water. Have students make drawings to document all of the shapes they observe in their math journals. For example, put water in a rectangular prism and see if they can make the surface of the water form a triangle, a rectangle, a pentagon, and so on.

Making Slices (Handout 6A)

Directions: Read the instructions for making slices below. Draw the appropriate slices on the back of this page or on a blank sheet of paper.

1. A rectangular prism is 10 cm long, 3 cm deep, and 4 cm high. Imagine making five equally spaced cuts through it as pictured below. Draw the resulting five cross sections and label the dimensions.

    a. with slices made perpendicular to the table top and parallel to the shaded end:

    b. with slices made perpendicular to the table top and parallel to the long end:

    c. with slices made parallel to the table top:

2. A cone sits on a cutting board as shown. Draw the resulting five cross sections from slicing the cone:

    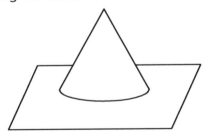

    a. with slices made perpendicular to the cutting board and parallel to the right edge of the table top.

    b. with slices made parallel to the cutting board.

    c. with slices made parallel to the slanted edge of the cone.

Name:_____ Date:_____

Slice the Apple (Handout 6B)

Directions: Read the instructions for making slices below. Draw the appropriate slices on the back of this page or a blank sheet of paper.

1. Imagine that a real apple with a bite out of it (similar to the picture below) sits on this page. Imagine what the resulting cross sections would look like if five equally spaced slices are made.

2. Draw the five slices if they are made parallel to the table top.

3. Draw the five slices if they are made from top to bottom of the apple, parallel to the right side of this page.

4. Draw the five slices if they are made from top to bottom of the apple, parallel to this sheet of paper.

Name:_____   Date:_____

Build the Mystery Solid (Handout 6C)

Directions: If you know what the cross sections look like, can you visualize the solid? Make the mystery solids described below.

1. Use the following clues to make the mystery solid out of playdough.

    a. The solid is 6 inches tall.

    b. The base of the solid is an equilateral triangle. (It sits on this base on the tabletop.)

    c. The cross sections of the mystery solid are slices that are made parallel to the tabletop. They are equilateral triangles that have edges the same length as the distance of the slice from the top of the solid.

2. Your friend, who lives 1,000 miles away, wants to know what the solid looks like. Draw it and write a detailed description of the solid on the back of this page or on a blank piece of paper.

Wrap and Slice (Handout 6D)

Directions: Follow the steps below to create slices of solids.

1. Make solids with your playdough as indicated in the chart.
2. Cut a strip of tissue paper and wrap it around each solid.
3. Make a cut with fishing line or dental floss as indicated.
4. Unwrap the tissue paper and sketch the shape of the paper along the cut line.
5. Change the angle of the cut and see what effect it has on the shape of the paper.

Make this solid.	Make a cut that looks like this.	Draw the tissue paper after it is unwrapped.
Long cylinder		
Rectangular prism with a square end		
Cone		

6. Choose one of the solids you made. On the back of this page or a blank piece of paper, write a paragraph explaining the effect of the cutting angle on the shape of the paper when it is unwrapped.

Lesson 7: Solids of Revolution

Instructional Purpose

- To visualize three-dimensional objects that are created by revolving a two-dimensional shape around an axis

Materials and Handouts

- Paper Shapes (Handout 7A)
- Solids of Revolution (Handout 7B)
- Solids of Revolution Answer Key (Teacher Resource 1)
- Revolve It! (Handout 7C)
- Revolve It! Answer Key (Teacher Resource 2)
- Straws or pencils
- Scissors
- Tape
- Calculators

Activities

1. Review the x-y coordinate plane as a class. Tell students that it was developed by the French mathematician, René Descartes (1596–1650). Legend says that he was lying in bed watching a fly walking on the ceiling, and he developed this coordinate system as a way to describe the location of the fly.

2. Give students Paper Shapes (Handout 7A), straws, and tape. They should cut the shapes from the page. Then, have them make a slit in the straw and insert the paper circle in the slit. Have them spin the straw in the palms of their hands to give the impression of the solid formed by the revolution. Repeat for the other shapes. Tell students that if a two-dimensional figure revolves around the x- or y-axis then a solid is formed. Tell students that these are called *solids of revolution* in calculus.

3. Distribute a copy of Solids of Revolution (Handout 7B) and display a transparency copy on the overhead projector. Have students predict what the solid of revolution will be for each of the figures. Debrief about each one before moving onto the next question. Encourage students to use their paper shapes and straw to demonstrate the solids of revolution.

4. Distribute Revolve It! (Handout 7C) and have students complete it. Encourage them to make models with straws and paper shapes.

5. Debrief student answers.

Note to Teacher

1. The following is background information on the formulas for volume and surface area of a cylinder. You may use these ideas to make a visual demonstration for your students.

a. Volume of cylinder = πr²h: Assuming students know that the area of a circle is πr^2, you can think of the cylinder as a stack of circles. The formula for volume is the area of the base times the height of the cylinder. You might use old CDs to stack up as a visual construction.

b. Surface area of a cylinder = $(2\pi r)h + 2(\pi r^2)$: Think about a soup can. If you take off the label and flatten it, it is a rectangle with length equal to the circumference of the top of the can and width equal to the height of the can. The surface area of the can is the area of this rectangle plus the areas of the circular top and bottom of the can.

Assessment

- Revolve It! (Handout 7C)

Resources

- "Generating Solids," by Evan Maletsky, *The Mathematics Teacher*, October 1983 pp. 499–500, 505–507. Worksheets are provided to help students visualize, identify, and describe the solids generated by rotating polygons about axes in various positions, to relate these figures to cylinders and cones, and to compute their surface areas and volumes.

Paper Shapes (Handout 7A)

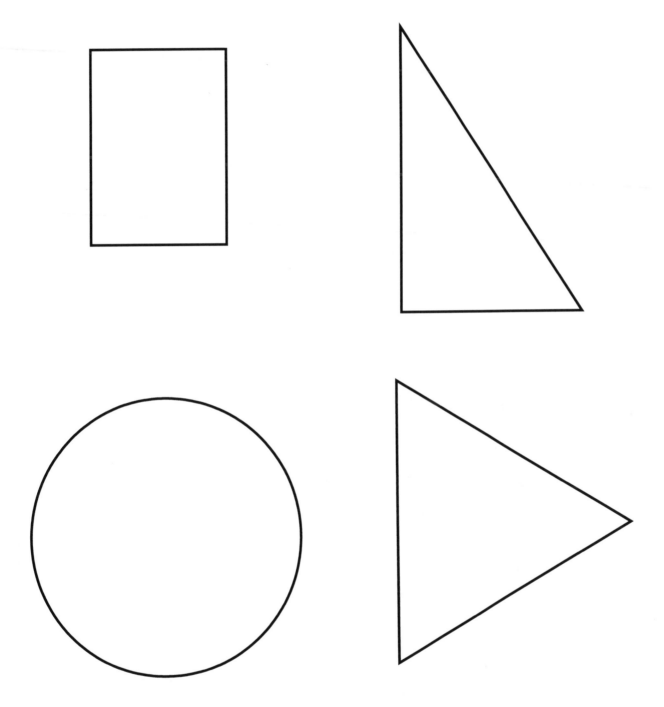

Solids of Revolution (Handout 7B)

	Draw the solid.	Describe the solid in words.
(circle, $r = 3$)		
(rectangle, 2 by 4)		
(triangle, 2 and 3)		
(triangle, 2 and 3)		
(triangle, 2 and 3)		

Solids of Revolution Answer Key
(Teacher Resource 1)

	Draw the solid.	Describe the solid in words.
		Sphere with radius three units, centered at the origin
		Cylinder with radius four units and height two units
		Cone with radius three units and height two units
		Looks like a cylinder with radius three units with an inverted cone cut out; the radius of the base of the cone is three units and the height is two units
		Cone with vertex on the x axis with radius of 2 units and height 3 units

Revolve It! (Handout 7C)

Directions: Each shaded area is revolved around the indicated axis. Draw the resulting solid the best that you can and describe it in words.

	Revolve the given area around the x-axis.	**Revolve the given area around the y-axis.**

Revolve It! Answer Key
(Teacher Resource 2)

	Revolve the given area around the x-axis.	Revolve the given area around the y-axis.
	Cylinder with height seven units and radius three units	Cylinder with height three units and radius seven units
	Cylinder with height four units and radius one unit	Washer with outer radius 6 units and inner radius 2 units; or shallow cylinder of height 1 unit and radius 6 units with a smaller cylinder of the same weight and radius 2 units removed from the center.
	Cone with vertex at the origin; height is seven units; radius of the base is three units.	Cylinder of radius seven and height three units with an inverted cone cut out of it.

Lesson 8: Sierpinski Triangle and Pyramid

Instructional Purpose

- To introduce the idea of fractals
- To explore a two-dimensional and three-dimensional version of Sierpinski fractals

Materials and Handouts

- Sierpinski Triangle (Handout 8A)
- Sierpinski Area (Handout 8B)
- Sierpinski Area Answer Key (Teacher Resource 1)
- Scrap paper
- Two envelopes per student, approximately 3.5 inches by 6.5 inches

Vocabulary

- **Fractal:** A geometric shape that can be split into parts, each of which is (at least approximately) a reduced-size copy of the whole
- **Iteration:** One cycle of a set of instructions to be repeated
- **Self-similarity:** An object is similar to a part of itself; the whole has the same shape as one or more of the parts

Activities

1. Explain that fractals are geometric patterns that are repeated at smaller scales to produce irregular shapes and surfaces that cannot be represented by classical geometry. It involves the idea of iteration, in which a cycle of operations is repeated, and the idea of self-similarity, in which an image is similar (same shape) as the previous shape but proportionally larger or smaller. In a fractal pattern, the basic pattern is iterated using smaller versions of the pattern that are all similar to each other and the original. It means that the object looks the same no matter what power magnifying glass you use to view it.

2. Show students an example of a fractal known as the Koch Snowflake. Distribute scrap paper. Demonstrate on the overhead projector and have students try it on their papers using a pencil.
   a. Start with a large equilateral triangle.
   b. Divide one side of the triangle into three equal parts and remove the middle section. Replace it with two lines the same length as the section you removed, creating an outward extension of the perimeter. Do this to all three sides of the triangle.
   c. Do it again and again to each new segment of the figure. If you do it infinitely, you have a fractal. Each round is called an iteration. Each new construction is self-similar. Figure 16 shows the iterations of the Koch Snowflake.

Figure 16. Iterations of the Koch Snowflake.

3. Distribute Sierpinski Triangle (Handout 8A) and have students work in groups to complete it. Tell students that usually the center triangle is cut out, as shown in Figure 17, in the first four stages of a Sierpinski Triangle. Because it is awkward for students to cut out the centers, they will be shading the centers and leaving the three triangles surrounding it blank. The results are the same with opposite color patterns.

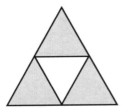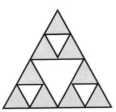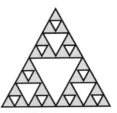

Figure 17. Sierpinski Triangle.

4. Have the students discuss their answers. Distribute Sierpinski Area (Handout 8B) and have students complete it. Discuss their answers.

5. Tell students to now think of fractals three-dimensionally, as in the Sierpinski Pyramid. Help students make tetrahedrons from envelopes and assemble the pyramid by telling them the following directions.
   a. Hold the flap up on the envelope as shown in Figure 18. On the back of the envelope, draw both diagonals AC and BD.

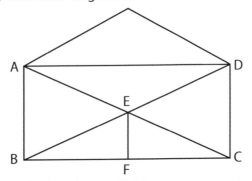

Figure 18. Orientation of the envelope for Sierpinski Pyramid project.

   b. Cut out the top quarter of the envelope by cutting along AE and ED.
   c. Crease the remaining envelope along FE by folding in half. Fold in both directions for a sharp crease. Unfold and lay it flat.
   d. Crease the envelope along EC and BE. Fold in both directions for a sharp crease. Unfold and lay it flat.

e. Pull the back and front of the envelope away from each other to open it up. Insert corner D into the interior of the opposite side of the envelope, toward corner F, until the two parts form a tetrahedron.

f. Ask students the following questions.
   i. What is the resulting solid called? (A tetrahedron)
   ii. What are the characteristics of a tetrahedron? (Four faces that are triangles)
   iii. What does the term regular tetrahedron imply? (All faces are equilateral triangles)

6. Tell students that now they are going to build a three-dimensional fractal using the tetrahedrons they have made. Do an Internet search using the term "Sierpinski Pyramid" in order to show students pictures of various pyramid stages.

   a. Have groups of four students tape together four tetrahedrons to look like Figure 19. Call the new structure a stage 1 tetrahedron. Have four groups tape their stage 1 structure together to make a stage 2 tetrahedron. Point out to students that each of these is self-similar to the stage before it. Have students keep doing this until you run out of envelopes or space in the classroom. Tell students the result is called a Sierpinski Pyramid.

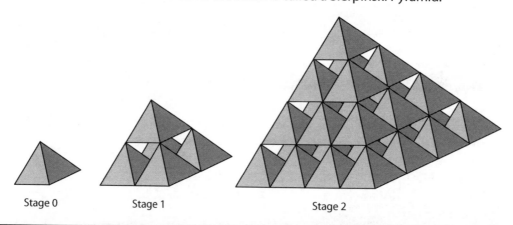

Stage 0   Stage 1   Stage 2

Figure 19. Stages of the Sierpinski Pyramid.

   b. Draw the table in Figure 20 on your chalkboard and have students complete it in order to determine how many stages to build. Students can cut and fold envelopes to save instructional time.

Stage	Number of envelopes needed	Estimate the height of the structure
0	1	
1	4	
2	16	
3		
4		
5		
6		

Figure 20. Data table to record Sierpinski Pyramid stages.

7. Have students write a comparison of the Sierpinski Triangle and Sierpinski Pyramid in their math journals or notebooks.

8. Have students study the stage 1 pyramid. Ask students: If a stage 0 pyramid, the tetrahedron made from one envelope, represents one unit of volume, can they then estimate the volume of the shaded space in the middle of the stage 1 pyramid? Have students share their estimates and discuss their thinking. (4. You can use a theorem from geometry that states: If the edge of a polyhedron [3-D analogue to a polygon] is increased by a factor of n, the volume is increased by a factor of n^3. In this case the edge of the stage 0 model is one unit of length and the edge of stage 1 is doubled, therefore the volume is 2^3 or 8 times as large. You can see four units of volume represented by the envelope tetrahedrons, so there must be four more accounted for in the interior blank space.)

Notes to Teacher

1. The ratio of length to width of the envelope determines whether the resulting tetrahedron is regular. If you use a #10 business envelope, the resulting solid will be an oblique triangular pyramid (it leans to one side).

2. It is important to use sharp creases.

Assessment

- Sierpinski Triangle (Handout 8A)
- Sierpinski Area (Handout 8B)
- Have students address the following prompt in a math journal: Image the silhouette of a very old tree in winter against the sky. Explain how the pattern of the tree branches resembles a fractal.

Extension

1. Have students learn more about fractals at the following Web site: http://math.rice.edu/~lanius/frac. Each student might choose a different fractal and make a presentation to the class.

Sierpinski Triangle (Handout 8A)

Directions: Follow the steps below to create a Sierpinski Triangle.

1. To make this fractal pattern on the dot paper, begin by drawing an equilateral triangle that is 16 units on each side (17 dots). This step is done for you below in the diagram.

2. Mark the midpoints of the sides of the triangle and connect them with line segments.

3. Shade in the middle "upside-down" triangle.

4. For each of the three remaining equilateral triangles, mark the midpoints of the sides of the triangle and connect them with line segments.

5. Shade the middle triangle created in each new triangle.

6. Mark the midpoints of the sides of the remaining triangles and connect them with line segments.

7. If you continue this process forever, the result is called a Sierpinski Triangle.

Sierpinski Area (Handout 8B)

Directions: Follow the steps below to find the area of a Sierpinski Triangle.

1. Assume that the original triangle has an area of one square unit. Find the area that is shaded after each iteration and enter it in the table below.

Iteration	Fraction of original triangle that is shaded after this iteration
0	0
1	¼
2	
3	
4	

2. Predict what fraction of the original triangle would be shaded if you shaded triangles in the fifth iteration. Explain how you made your prediction.

_____

_____

_____

_____

3. If you continued this process forever, what fraction of the original triangle would be shaded?

_____

_____

_____

_____

_____

Sierpinski Area Answer Key
(Teacher Resource 1)

Directions: Follow the steps below to find the area of a Sierpinski Triangle.

1. Assume that the original triangle has an area of one square unit. Find the area that is shaded after each iteration and enter it in the table.

Iteration	Fraction of original triangle that is shaded after this iteration
0	0
1	¼
2	¼ + ³⁄₁₆ = ⁷⁄₁₆
3	¼ + ³⁄₁₆ + ⁹⁄₆₄ = ³⁷⁄₆₄
4	¼ + ³⁄₁₆ + ⁹⁄₆₄ + ²⁷⁄₂₅₆ = ¹⁷⁵⁄₂₅₆

2. Predict what fraction of the original triangle would be shaded if you shaded triangles in the fifth iteration. Explain how you made your prediction.

   175/256 + 81/1024 = 781/1024

3. If you continued this process forever, what fraction of the original triangle would be shaded?

   All of it; the fractions are getting closer and closer to one, but they will never go higher than one.

Lesson 9: Postassessment

Instructional Purpose

- To review the major concepts of the unit
- To administer the postassessment for the unit

Materials and Handouts

- Nets (Handout 9A)
- Postassessment (Handout 9B)
- Postassessment Answer Key (Teacher Resource 1)
- Isometric dot paper
- Square grid paper

Activities

1. Distribute Nets (Handout 9A) and have students work in groups to complete it.

2. Distribute the Postassessment (Handout 9A) and have students complete it individually. Collect and score the assessments using the Postassessment Answer Key (Teacher Resource 1).

3. Have students compare their preassessment to their postassessment responses. Reflect about what they have learned and how they have grown as mathematicians throughout the course of the unit.

Note to Teacher

1. The postassessment is parallel in structure to the preassessment for this unit. Change any sets of questions to mirror any changes you made in the preassessment.

Nets (Handout 9A)

Directions: There are many ways to give information about three-dimensional objects in two dimensions. The pattern below is called a net. Cut it out and tape it together to form a triangular prism. Then use it to answer the questions that follow.

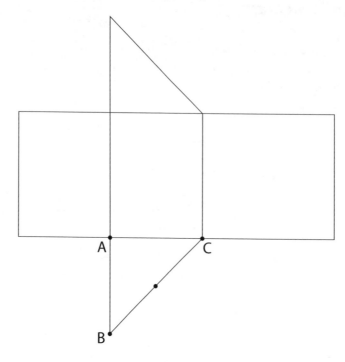

1.   In the triangular prism you constructed, the triangular bases are isosceles right triangles.

2.   Set the prism in this orientation with the largest rectangular face on the tabletop.

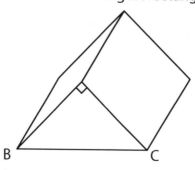

3.   Draw the three orthogonal projections on the back of this page or a blank piece of paper:

    a.   the top view

    b.   the front view

    c.   the right side view

4. Think about making four slices that are parallel to the triangular face. Draw the images of the slices.

5. Think about making four slices that are parallel to line segment BC. Draw the images of the slices.

6. On the grid below build a structure using 14 one-inch cubes. Every cube must be joined to at least one other cube at a face, not a corner. You must stack the cubes so that faces touch each other exactly (with no overhanging or rotated cubes).

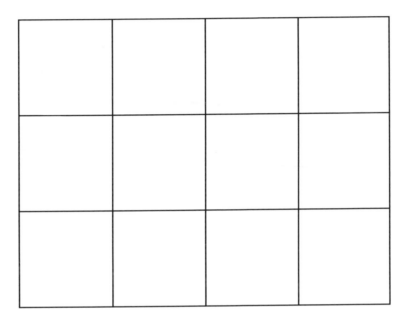

7. Make a mat plan for your structure.

8. Draw a picture of the structure on isometric dot paper.

9. Draw a picture of the structure on the square grid paper.

10. Draw the following orthogonal projections on the back of this page or a blank piece of paper: top view, front view, and right side view.

11. Ask a classmate to build your structure from your projections.

Postassessment (Handout 9B)

Directions: Do your best to answer the following questions.

1. Construct a building with cubes by placing the given number of cubes on each square.

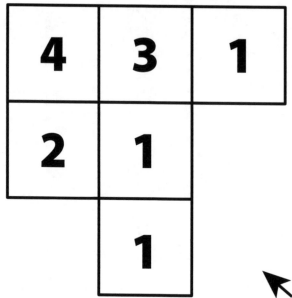

2. Draw a picture of the building below as it looks from the corner marked with the arrow. You may use the dot paper or the back of this page to draw your picture.

3. On the back of this page or a blank piece of paper, draw the following three views of the building in #1 above:

 a. the top view

 b. the front view

 c. the right side

4. Give an example of each of the following:

 a. one-dimensional object _____

 b. two-dimensional object _____

 c. three-dimensional object _____

5. How many cubes are needed to build this building? Show your work.

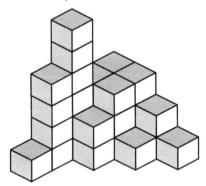

6. What is a fractal?

 _____

 _____

 _____

7. A roll of wrapping paper is cut with a knife at the angle shown. If the paper is unwrapped, what does the shaded piece look like? Draw it.

8. A pyramid with a square base is made of playdough. Maria said she cut the pyramid by passing a knife through points A, B, and C. Draw the shape of the cross section.

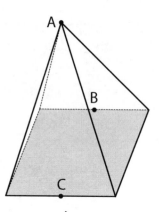

9. Josh said he cut the pyramid by passing a knife through points M, N, and P. Draw the shape of the cross section.

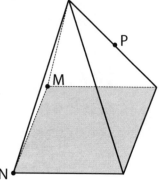

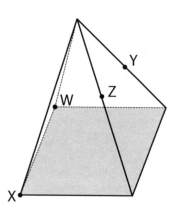

10. Elmo said he cut the pyramid by passing a knife through points W, X, Y, and Z. Draw the shape of the cross section.

Extra Challenge Questions:

1. Imagine a building made with cubes that are placed as shown below in the diagram. Do not build the building.

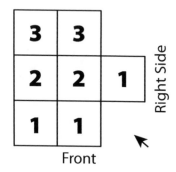

2. Draw a picture of the building as it looks from the corner marked with the arrow. You may use the dot paper below or the blank space to draw your picture.

3. On the back of this page or on a blank piece of paper, draw the following three views of the building in #1 above:

   a. the top view

   b. the front view

   c. the right side view

Postassessment Answer Key
(Teacher Resource 1)

Directions: Do your best to answer the following questions.

1. Construct a building with cubes by placing the given number of cubes on each square.

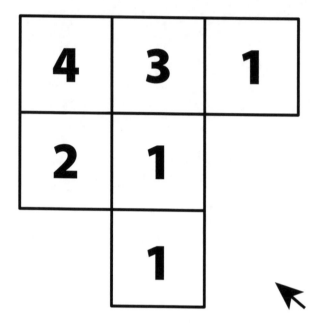

2. Draw a picture of the building below as viewed from the corner marked with the arrow. You may use the dot paper or the blank space to draw your picture.

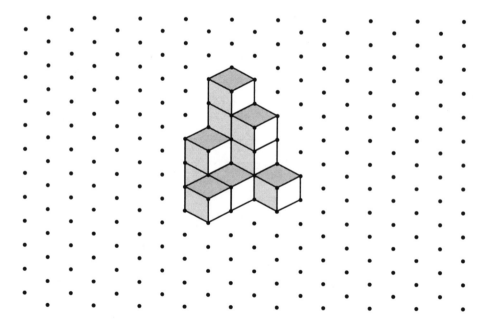

3. On the back of this page or a blank piece of paper, draw the following three views of the building in #1 above:

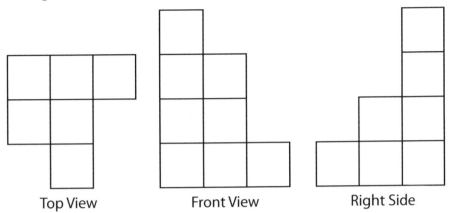

Top View   Front View   Right Side

4. Give an example of each of the following:

   a. one-dimensional object

   A line on a piece of paper, or other similar example

   b. a two-dimensional object

   A rectangle drawn on a piece of paper, a picture of something, and so on

   c. a three-dimensional object

   A box of cereal, a pencil, or any other object that can be picked up

5. How many cubes are needed to build this building? Show your work.

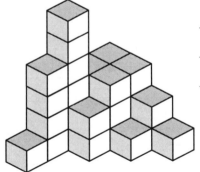

29; one way to find out is to count the number

of cubes in each tower, write the number on top

of the tower, and then add the numbers

6. What is a fractal?

   The response should be similar to this:

   A fractal is a geometric pattern that can be split into parts, each of which is

   (at least approximately) a reduced-size copy of the whole.

7. A roll of wrapping paper is cut with a knife at the angle shown. If the paper is unwrapped, what does the shaded piece look like? Draw it.

8. A pyramid with a square base is made of playdough. Maria said she cut the pyramid by passing a knife through points A, B, and C. Draw the shape of the cross section.

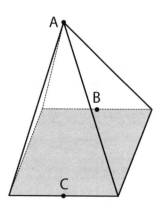

9. Josh said he cut the pyramid by passing a knife through points M, N, and P. Draw the shape of the cross section.

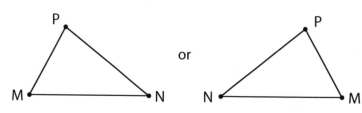

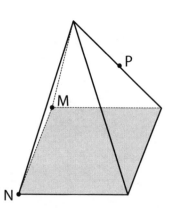

10. Elmo said he cut the pyramid by passing a knife through points W, X, Y, and Z. Draw the shape of the cross section.

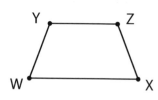

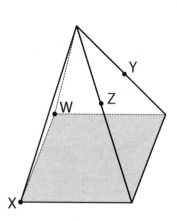

Extra Challenge Questions:

1. Imagine a building made with cubes that are placed as shown below in the diagram. Do not actually build the building.

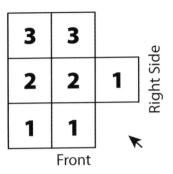

2. Draw a picture of the building as it looks from the corner marked with the arrow. You may use the dot paper below or the blank space to draw your picture.

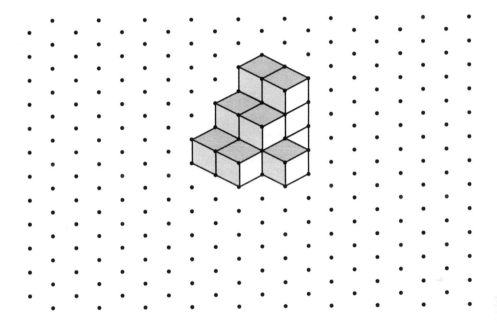

3. On the back of this page or on a blank piece of paper, draw the following three views of the building in #1 above:

   a. the top view

   b. the front view

   c. the right side view

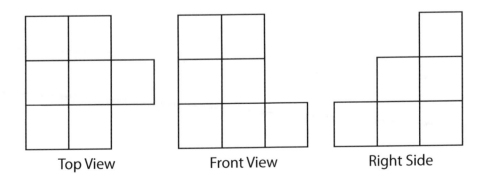

Top View   Front View   Right Side

Part III:
Unit Extensions

Unit Extensions

1. Get a copy of "Spatial Visualization" by Glenda Lappan, Elizabeth A. Phillips, and Mary Jean Winter, in the November 1984 issue of *The Mathematics Teacher*, pp. 618–625. (You may need to visit a library or find a teacher with a current subscription to the magazine to access a copy.) Worksheets are included that ask students to:
   a. Copy pictures of solids on isometric dot paper.
   b. Imagine that a certain cube is removed from a cube structure and draw the remaining structure.
   c. Draw different corner views of solids.
   d. Put two cube structures together to form a new one.

2. Have students tie an overhand knot in a strip of paper, being careful to tighten it slowly, and flatten it as it gets tight. See the diagram below. If you snip off the excess paper, it forms a pentagon. Ask students the following questions (see http://www.jimloy.com/geometry/pentagon.htm for some hints).
   a. Is it a regular pentagon?
   b. Can you prove that it is a regular pentagon?

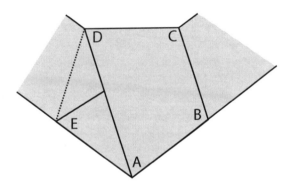

3. Without measuring, have students find the length of the diagonal of a shoebox.

4. Have students search online for the Johns Hopkins University Spatial Test Battery (STB) Web site. Have them try the samples.

5. Have students find the sample Dental Admissions Test online and try the section on spatial reasoning.

6. Ask students: If the faces of a tetrahedron are equilateral triangles congruent to the triangular faces of a pyramid with square base, then how many faces does a polyhedron have that is created by gluing them together at a triangular face so that the vertices of the triangles coincide? (The easiest way to see the answer is to build the tetrahedron and the square-based pyramid. At first one might guess seven faces, as two faces vanish. But the polyhedron has only five faces, as two rhombi are created. You can model this easily with Polydrons™.)

7. Have students play Cootie Catcher Contest.
   a. Part I: Making Cootie Catchers
      i. Either make two "Cootie Catchers" for each student in advance or have students make them. Label one with the numbers and letters as described below. Keep the other one blank.
      ii. Start with a square piece of paper. Fold and crease along both diagonals.
      iii. Unfold so you are back to the square.
      iv. Fold each corner point into the center of the square. The result should be a smaller square.
      v. Flip it over and fold all four corners points into the center again. The result is another smaller square.
      vi. Fold a pair of opposite sides of the square together and crease.
      vii. Open and repeat with other pair of sides.
      viii. On the side with the triangular flaps, write the numbers 1 to 8 on each of the small triangles like this with numbers all facing toward the center

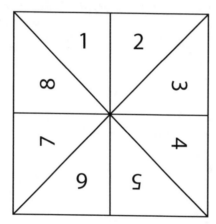

      ix. Then open the flaps and write the letters A to H so that the letters correspond with the numbers (A-1, B-2, etc.) with letters all facing to the center.

   b. Part II: Contest Directions
      i. Students need one labeled Cootie Catcher.
      ii. Give them 1 minute to study the Cootie Catcher that is labeled. The only movement allowed is to lift the labeled flaps and close them again to see how the movement works. (You may call this one the model.)
      iii. Collect the labeled Cootie Catchers.
      iv. Give students a blank Cootie Catcher and have them unfold it all the way and lay it out flat.
      v. Tell students to label the blank Cootie Catcher with the letters A to H and numbers 1 to 8 so that it would match the model when folded. They may not fold the paper! The only legal moves of the paper are to rotate it on the desk or flip the whole paper over. Give them one minute to complete this task.
      vi. Disqualify anyone from the contest who folds the paper.
      vii. Have students sign their names along the edge of their solution.
      viii. Have students exchange their solutions.
      ix. Return a model to each student and have him or her use it to score the solution of the partner.

c. Points for Scoring:
    i. Numbers:
        1. 1 point for each number in the correct location.
        2. 1 point for each number in the correct orientation.
    ii. Letters:
        1. 1 point for each letter in the correct location.
        2. 1 point for each number in the correct orientation.
    iii. The winner has the largest number of points.

Common Core State Standards Alignment

Lesson	Common Core State Standards in Math
Lesson 1: Preassessment	6.G.A Solve real-world and mathematical problems involving area, surface area, and volume.
	7.G.A Draw construct, and describe geometrical figures and describe the relationships between them.
Lesson 2: Introduction to Dimensions	6.G.A Solve real-world and mathematical problems involving area, surface area, and volume.
Lesson 3: Drawing Cube Structures	6.G.A Solve real-world and mathematical problems involving area, surface area, and volume.
Lesson 4: Projecting Solids Into Two Dimensions	6.G.A Solve real-world and mathematical problems involving area, surface area, and volume.
	7.G.A Draw construct, and describe geometrical figures and describe the relationships between them.
	HSG-GMD.B Visualize relationships between two-dimensional and three-dimensional objects.
Lesson 5: Polycubes	6.G.A Solve real-world and mathematical problems involving area, surface area, and volume.
Lesson 6: Slices	7.G.A Draw construct, and describe geometrical figures and describe the relationships between them.
	HSG-GMD.B Visualize relationships between two-dimensional and three-dimensional objects.
Lesson 7: Solids of Revolution	6.G.A Solve real-world and mathematical problems involving area, surface area, and volume.
	7.G.B Solve real-life and mathematical problems involving angle measure, area, surface area, and volume.
	8.G.C Solve real-world and mathematical problems involving volume of cylinders, cones, and spheres.
	HSG-GMD.B Visualize relationships between two-dimensional and three-dimensional objects.
Lesson 8: Sierpinski Triangle and Pyramid	6.G.A Solve real-world and mathematical problems involving area, surface area, and volume.
	7.G.B Solve real-life and mathematical problems involving angle measure, area, surface area, and volume.
	8.G.A Understand congruence and similarity using physical models, transparencies, or geometry software.
Lesson 9: Postassessment	6.G.A Solve real-world and mathematical problems involving area, surface area, and volume.
	7.G.A Draw construct, and describe geometrical figures and describe the relationships between them.